Nelson Gets a Fright

Story by Beverley Randell
Illustrations by Julian Bruère

Nelson, the baby elephant,
lived in Africa with his mother
and his grandmother
and his aunts and his cousins
and his big sister Nina.
Nelson was six months old.
Every day, he drank lots of milk
from his mother.

He was learning to eat grass
and leaves, too,
and he used his soft little trunk
to smell everything.

3

Nelson watched his mother
as she pulled up grass with her trunk
and put it into her mouth.
Nelson tried and tried,
but he couldn't tear the grass.
His trunk was not big enough
or strong enough.

In the end, he got down on his knees
and put his mouth around the grass
and tried to **bite** it off.
He was only a baby elephant!

Nelson liked playing games
with his cousins and his big sister Nina.
Sometimes they pushed each other.
Sometimes they chased each other
through the grass.

Nelson liked chasing wildebeest, too.
He would run up to them
and flap his big ears,
and the wildebeest would run away.
This made Nelson feel
very big and strong.
Nothing frightened **him**!

7

One day, when Nelson and Nina
had been chasing wildebeest,
Nelson saw something
lying in the grass.
He ran over to see what it was.

That was a big mistake!

The something in the grass
was a lioness!
She stood up in front of Nelson.
He turned to go back,
but another lioness was there,
right behind him. And another!

The lionesses were between Nelson
and his big sister Nina.
Nelson tried to run somewhere else,
but there were lionesses all around him,
blocking his way.

The lionesses were hungry.
They had not eaten for two days,
and they had cubs to feed.
They all came closer to Nelson.
They were going to spring on his back.

Nelson was very frightened.
He bellowed
as he tried to run past the lionesses.
Nina cried out, too.

Nelson's mother and grandmother
and aunts and cousins heard the cries,
and they all came charging
to the rescue.
They lifted up their trunks
and trumpeted as they ran.

The ground shook as the herd rushed to save Nelson.

The lionesses heard them coming. They turned and fled.

Nelson and Nina ran towards the herd.

And for a long time afterwards,
they did not play **too** far away
from their family.